JOURNEY

ZANE PARKS

Lulu.com

"For Those in Peril" and "Dear Coz" originally appeared in **Mariposa**; "Korea," "3rd Sunday Singin'," "Home for the Holidays," "Visiting Family in West Virginia" and "Mozart's Birthday" originally appeared in **Frogpond**; "Honey," "Hank," "Bounce," "Lost and Found," "A Private Affair" and "Depth Perception" originally appeared in **Simply Haiku**; "Accident" originally appeared in **Haiku Harvest**; "Private Language," "One Brass Knuckle," "Bob," "Road Trip," "Nine Eleven," "Seasons," "Submission" and "A Friend in Need" originally appeared in **Contemporary Haibun Online**; "I Swear," "Mimi," "My First Ex-wife's Best Friend," "Buddy," "Commute" and "Come the Revolution" originally appeared in **Lynx**; "First Banana Split" and "Just Deserts" originally appeared in **bottle rockets**; "Odious Explosion," "Easter Chicks" and "Anna" originally appeared in **Ink Sweat & Tears**; "New Catalog," "Rite of Passage" and "Winter's Approach" originally appeared in **Chrysanthemum Haiku Journal**; "Looking Back" originally appeared in **Blithe Spirit**; "Double Date," "Coolness," "A New Day" and "Needs" originally appeared in **Modern Haiku**; "Not Too Swift," "Portrait of the Artist," "Double Jeopardy" and "The Interview" originally appeared in **paper wasp**; "Celebration," "The Professor," "Pièce de Résistance" and "Beach House" originally appeared in **Stylus Poetry Journal**; "Holidays" originally appeared in **Raw Nervz**; "Keys" originally appeared in **Kokako**; "Anniversary Getaway" originally appeared in **Shamrock Haiku Journal**.

ISBN: 978-1-67817-992-2

In Loving Memory of

Mimi

Preface

The poems in this collection are *haibun*, a form unfamiliar to many. It originated in Japan and is defined by the Haiku Society of America (see http://www.hsa-haiku.org/archives/HSA_Definitions_2004.html) as follows:

> A haibun is a terse, relatively short prose poem in the haikai style, usually including both lightly humorous and more serious elements. A haibun usually ends with a haiku.

It was first used in the travel writings of Bashō. Bashō is often thought of as the father of haiku. *Haikai* is a Japanese style of linked verse, but can also refer to diaries and travel writing.

The magazine *Contemporary Haibun Online* (http://contemporaryhaibunonline.com/pages_all/haibundefinitions.html) defines haibun as follows:

> Contemporary haibun is a combination of prose and haiku poetry, sometimes described as 'a narrative of epiphany'. Like English haiku, English haibun is evolving as it becomes more widely practiced in the English speaking world.

There is much elaboration and many examples on their website.

So much for the form, what of the content?

When my father was finishing up at the seminary, he began to do supply preaching, that is, filling in for a preacher while he was away on vacation, and then, trial preaching, that is, preaching for a church that is looking for a preacher. Because each church was different, Dad could and did use the same sermon. As we drove to each of these churches we would groan when we realized that once again Dad would be giving the sermon, "Salvation, a Journey." In that sermon, he likened salvation to a journey. While these haibun are not about salvation, they are about life, which might we be likened to a journey. Most of these poems are moments in my own journey.

Contents

For Those in Peril

We knew the risk going in. It's a hard thing to know the hour of your death. Harder yet to have a hand in it. Well, it's not as if we can not die. We just have a choice in the manner. Slowly as the oxygen in this chamber is depleted or more quickly drowning. We vote to open 'er up and let the water in.

> fireflies
> in a mason jar
> slowly flicker out

Honeymoon

Early August. Young lovers. A brilliant flash. A shattering roar. Their bodies melt into each other.

      reading the stories
      of saddam's war crimes
      a-bomb day

Korea

Dad was a navy pilot. During the Korean War, he served on an aircraft carrier. He did aerial reconnaissance. The planes for that had little or no armament. Fighters accompanied them for protection. Another pilot was sick and Dad's best friend volunteered for the mission. When MIGs appeared, he was intent on completing the assignment. One last photograph.

winter coming
geese
close up a gap

Honey

As a very young child, I called my mother "Honey." I heard Dad call her that and followed suit. Mom thought it was cute and encouraged it. I can imagine another kid's blank look when I asked, "Is your honey home?" The practice stopped abruptly when I started grammar school. You know how cruel children can be.

> school playground
> staring at the boy
> with buck teeth

Accident

Just a kid. Riding my bike. A funny noise. The chain?
Looking down, bam! A parked car. The handle bar twists into
my groin. On the ground, I can barely breathe, barely move.
Slowly crawl home. Over lawns, sidewalks, street.

Mom checks me out. Just a spot of blood. It's not so bad. She
tucks me into bed. I get to stay home the next day. My
friends come by after school. It's kinda funny. They each give
me a dime. But man, that's cool. A dime is a new comic book.

    weekday morning
    I watch a mouse
    save the day

Private Language

We're going on a winkidink. That's what my little brother calls
a picnic. There are public bathrooms but they're pretty rank.
Mom won't use them at all. We just use them to pee. None of
us would use them for tootilitot.

> cat's plaintive cry
> the bug just
> out of reach

I Swear

I'm in the 3ʳᵈ grade, Jimmy's in the 4ᵗʰ. We fight coming home from school. I swear. I just start cussing and say things I don't mean. Why did I call his mother a bitch? I like her. Jeez, she's one of the sweetest moms on the block. I tell my own mom, "The fight wasn't *about* anything. It was just a fight." I hope Jimmy keeps his mouth shut. Maybe he doesn't even look like he was in a fight.

> the new clock's charm
> fades around midnight
> cuckoo

First Banana Split

On the way home from school, my friend wants to stop by the drug store. He orders a banana split. I watch in awe as he eats it. Not a penny in my pocket.

At home, a quick "Hi, Mom." I run to my grandmother and standby her wheelchair. "Oh, Mimi," I begin wistfully. "I saw the neatest thing today." I tell her of this wondrous concoction and my desperate need. She has little enough to call her own, but those gnarled fingers I know and love so well reach into her coin purse, count out the cost.

I race to the drug store. Proudly order one for myself. I jab my spoon in with enthusiasm. The dish goes flying. My beautiful banana split a wreck on the floor. I fly home in tears. Again the purse, again the coins. With a firm grip on the dish, I devour this one with gusto.

> my new baby boy
> the crook of her arm
> just the right nook

Mimi

My mother's mother was named Willie Mae. All her grandchildren knew her as Mimi. I have dim memories of her trying to walk on crutches. But mostly I remember her in a wheelchair. Her arms and legs bent. Her hands and fingers gnarled. No touch more gentle and loving. She lived with us off and on throughout my childhood. Her love was the sweetest kind – unconditional.

> foggy morning
> wafting from the church
> amazing grace

One Brass Knuckle

He was proud of his college ring. First in the family to graduate. I knew the ring differently. Felt it on the back of my head. I got between him and the TV. Smack! Licking my plate at dinner. Smack! A buck tooth chipped to boot.

> homecoming
> watching the game
> with dad
> I root for
> the underdog

Odious Explosion

Right in the middle of social studies class, I fart. Loudly. I'm mortified. A moment of stunned silence. But then relief. The class clown claims it as his own. Everybody laughs.

cat on the mantle
I catch the buddha
in his fall

Easter Chicks

My brother and I get Easter chicks. Down so soft. Dyed pastels – one purple, one blue. One day they are no longer chicks.

"They're hateful. They peck my feet when I'm hanging the wash," Mom complains.

Then the ultimatum. "They go or I go."

At dinner, Dad says that some of the under feathers still showed the original dye. My brother grabs a drumstick, but I can't eat.

> mom happy
> with the new craze
> pet rocks

3rd Sunday Singin'

It's the 3rd Sunday in August. Gospel groups from all over come here to perform. As soon as the regular church service is over, Mom hurries us home to the parsonage. My folks don't rightly approve of the goings on at the Singin'. Things get pretty raucous and that ain't right in the Lord's house. Still, Dad's the preacher and he has to have some presence. But the rest of us stay strictly away. After supper my brother and I sneak back toward the church to hear what's going on. I've never heard "Peace in the Valley" so loud, almost shrill. I hardly think somebody could hear it sung like that and think peace.

> washing dishes
> grandma softly hums
> old rugged cross

New Catalog

Visiting Dad's sister in West Virginia was like visiting a
foreign country. Aunt Mildred didn't have indoor plumbing.
There the males went to the mining site to use the communal
showers. A blast of water, soap up, another blast to rinse off.
Don't remember what the women did. And then the
outhouse.

> christmas coming
> excitedly paging
> the new catalog

Just Deserts

Eighth grade. Coach teaches my all-boy social studies class. In my other classes, the kids are smart and behave. Not this one. Coach's standard punishment for rowdiness is two from two thousand. That is, on a piece of paper, you start out with two thousand, subtract two, add one, subtract two, add one, and so on until you get to zero. To be done after school and handed in the next day. A friend and I decide to write these up in advance and sell them to our more trouble-prone classmates. The going price is ten cents. But what to do with such wealth?

> school lunch
> the coolness in my hand
> of an ice cream cup

Dear Coz

A Christmas visit. You were sixteen. I a couple of years younger. You were a beautiful child and now had blossomed. Early morning. We were decorating the tree. You stood on a chair to reach the upper parts. I handed up ornaments, wide-eyed as you leaned over to place them. Your baby doll pajama top swinging out.

      state fair
      dad hurries us past
      the girlie show tent

Looking Back

Woodruff, South Carolina. Early 1960s. Mom has a temporary job checking kids' eyesight at the colored school. One night she brings the equipment home to check my brother and me.

> vertigo
> in those first few steps
> new glasses

Double Date

"At least you're halfway decent looking," Paul says. He is homely as a mud fence. He's pretty much struck out with the girls at our high school. But Paul is resourceful. He's found a girl in a neighboring town. His girlfriend has a friend. Paul suggests we double date.

> drive-in movie
> the double feature
> under her sweater

Coolness

My folks won't spring for cool clothes like Weejuns, Gant shirts, a London Fog windbreaker. So, I take a job as a bag boy at the new Winn-Dixie. With the money earned I buy the windbreaker and shirts. But my feet are very narrow, triple-A. They just don't make Weejuns in my size.

> winter storm
> the trees sparkle
> in their icy coats

Not Too Swift

I've had a soft spot for her ever since our Senior class trip.
She sat next to me on that long train ride up to New York
City. She slept with her head on my shoulder. I know it's silly
to make anything of it, but there it is.

Months later, we're at a party. We go outside to be alone
together, to talk. Classmates drive up. Popular boys without
their girlfriends. They holler to her. "Come with us."

These are guys that make fun of her behind her back. "She's
not too swift." But she goes. My feelings a jumble.

    the preacher talks
    of mysterious ways
    things seen darkly

Portrait of the Artist

I'd seen her before, but running into her in the student union, I take her in. Her figure hourglass. Her long, blond hair baby-fine.

"I just finished my last final. Let's go get drunk," she says.

"I'd love to, but I'm broke."

"That's okay. I'll buy."

Guys hit on me, not on her. It's a gay bar. She's an art major. We talk music and the war.

> student garret
> a mirror captures
> the nude painting

Celebration

August 3, 1966. I'm twenty today. My roommate Mike has arranged everything – food, cake, beer. My girlfriend plans to stay over. We celebrate. Then Mike gives us the gift of privacy. Our first time.

>peace march
>we exchange the sign
>and the baby

Home for the Holidays

Late sixties. My wife and I wait with our small baby in our tiny student apartment. A bag packed. Mom and Dad are coming to take us home for the holidays. When they arrive, we sit and talk a bit. Then Dad goes out to the car and brings back our Christmas presents. I must have been confused. They've just come for a brief visit. When they leave, I realize they haven't seen me in a while. The beard and long hair.

> chemistry lab
> the boy with warts
> drops acid on them

My First Ex-wife's Best Friend

My wife's best friend is having trouble with her marriage.
She's coming to stay with us a bit. Our student apartment has
a single bed in the living room. That serves as a couch. She
can sleep there.

She's petit, pretty, engaging. My wife goes to bed early. The
two of us stay up talking, drinking beer.

> pretending
> innocence
> undone buttons

We play a board game. Sitting on the floor. Seeing a hint of
her breasts I am drawn closer. We kiss.

> scrabble tiles
> sticking to her
> bare skin

The Professor

Alan is widely liked and respected by colleagues and students.
There is that can of Fresca. Always with him. Some say it
might contain more than just Fresca. But no one makes much
of that. He's teaching a graduate seminar. In the middle of
the lecture, he collapses. Rushed to an emergency room. We
are all relieved when Alan comes back after a brief stay in the
hospital. As the seminar reconvenes, he says, "Now, where
was I?" and calmly lies down on the floor.

> cloudburst
> the tulip filling dips
> and bounces back

Anna

The fiercest of lovers. Even in sleep, she holds me tightly in her fist. As if to be sure she's wrung the last drop from me. When I've packed, she kneels offering her mouth. To delay my departure if only a little.

> the heat
> a bee nestles deeper
> in the pansy's pink folds

Hank

The last time I saw my cousin Hank, we were both young
men. He was stocky. I could easily imagine him playing high
school football; maybe a running back. In a flight of fancy, I
saw him as a local hero. With his rugged good looks, the girls
would've loved him. Those would have been his glory days.
Barring some great good fortune, he'd have gone to work in
the mines after graduation.

But Hank never spoke. It was softly said that perhaps the
doctor had misapplied forceps to his skull at birth. In that
time and place, doctors were gods. No one would have
thought to make a claim against one.

    in the road
    dark skid marks
    and fur darker still

Visiting Family in West Virginia

A good-looking, muscular young man in a football helmet. For him the helmet is a hateful thing. He wants it off, but lacks the understanding needed to unbuckle it. There is a makeshift dutch door that excludes access to the kitchen. Otherwise he has the run of the house. And run he does. But he doesn't unintentionally run into things. No more than you or I would. When he beats his head against the wall, you know he means it.

> checking out
> every nook and cranny
> new puppy

After supper the dishes are cleared and we drink coffee. Hank lunges for the dining table and we grab our cups. Not just to prevent spills. Hank loves coffee. He'll snatch and down your cup lickety-split if you're not on guard.

> waiting for
> the fog to lift
> morning tea

Now Uncle Junior holds Hank on his lap as a child. He takes off the helmet, speaks softly to him as a lover might. Words no one but Hank hears. He is calmed if only for a while. As we drive away, I wonder what my wife thinks. She talks of the love for Hank she saw in my uncle's eyes.

> coal mining town
> wet grimy streets
> and a rainbow

Forgiven

A gathering of cousins. Elderly women. Most haven't seen each other since they were girls in depression-era Alabama. One turns to my mother.

"Elizabeth, I forgive you."

"Why, Josephine, whatever for?" Mom asks.

"When we were children, you had silk drawers. Mine were sackcloth."

> pies in the oven
> she looks down on
> the empty flour sack

Mozart's Birthday

January 27th. It's the custom where I work to bring donuts on your
birthday. I bring them on Mozart's instead and stop by colleagues'
offices to let them know.

"Whose birthday?" asks a co-worker.

"Wolfgang Amadeus Mozart."

"Oh. Where does he sit?"

> birdsong
> I rub the crust from my eyes
> over toast

Roles

Big holiday meals are a family tradition. My wife does the bulk of the preparation. After dinner, the kids and I roll up our sleeves and put on the dishwashing symphony, Beethoven's 5th.

    cat paws pad
    around crystal goblets
    wine-stained linen

Pièce de Résistance

My wife's 50th birthday. Friends that cater take over the kitchen. I've selected the wine. We have a sauterne with salad. Aged bordeaux for the main course of beef wellington and asparagus with hollandaise sauce. For dessert, the pièce de résistance, a '63 vintage port. And the perfect accompaniment.

>dark chocolate sauce
>we lick each other's lips
>and spoon

Rite of Passage

I work alone late tonight. I'm consulting at the IT department of Elkerliek Ziekenhuis, a hospital in The Netherlands. When ready to leave, I discover that my usual exit is locked. I wander empty corridors until I come to what appears to be the hospital lobby. Again locked doors. Here I encounter what I had not thought to exist: a Dutch person that speaks no English. Somehow, he discerns my problem and points to a door I hadn't noticed. I try it and it opens. With a wave of gratitude toward my benefactor, I depart.

> leaving holland
> just now I see
> the windmills

Bob

Bob was a friend. A life-long friend to my wife. Sometimes they joked that she followed him. First from Bay City to Detroit and later to California. Bob found a home everywhere but finally in the gay community of San Francisco. There were visits back and forth through the years and more so toward the end. Visits to the hospital, visits to say goodbye. Every time he would recover. Every time but one. When he was gone, we gathered at his home. Filling plastic bags with unwanted, unneeded clothing to be given away.

> lightening the way
> to a goodwill store
> red feather boa

Road Trip

Driving south from Cape Town. As we near Cape Point,
traffic slows and then stops. A large family crosses the road in
single file. The very smallest carried by their mothers.
Baboons.

    hilltop lighthouse
    the waves of two oceans
    clashing

Bounce

My legs tire so quickly. The specialist attaches blood-pressure cuffs to my legs – thighs, calves, and tiny ones for the big toes. Cuffs inflate in synch. Diagnosis: arteries are clogged. Muscles aren't getting oxygen. In olden times, gangrene sets in and the legs are amputated. Nowadays it can be corrected with surgery. An aorta-femoral bypass graft. The surgeon shows me the part. An inverted Y. The top is a flexible cylinder with the circumference of a quarter. It splits into a couple of cylinders with the circumference of dimes. With the operation and time to recover, I will be back to normal.

> feeling it now
> I remember the bounce
> new tennis shoes

Nine Eleven

A colleague from our New York office is planning a training session to be held in the Twin Towers. She's having breakfast at Windows on the World.

For days hope remains alive. Everyone smiles seeing her walk into the office with her husband. But there's no answering smile. Now the realization, the weight of it. She has a twin. They've come to collect her things.

> hearing my name
> I turn
> to no one

Buddy

Buddy is very playful. We buy him the usual toys. The way he
chases and bats a rubber ball or toy mouse back and forth
across the room is a marvel. He fetches. He drops a ball near
me. I toss and he races for it. This repeats until one of us
tires. There's usually a collection of balls and mice under the
couch. Just out of reach. And feathers! Shake a stick with
feathers on it and he'll leap three feet.

But Buddy doesn't limit himself to bought toys. He's happy
playing with a discarded strip of plastic from the litter bucket.
Pens are fascinating on the counter. They must be knocked to
the floor. On the floor, they're uninteresting. He'll play with a
round bit of cardboard just the same as a ball or mouse. We
keep the feather duster out of sight.

> shoes slipped off
> what prey make you of
> these laces?

A New Day

She wakes in the morning and cries. It hurts so. The struggle
downstairs, coffee to brew, pills to take. This is a good day.
The alarm and not pain got her up. Soon caffeine, movement,
medication begin to take effect. Going upstairs isn't easy, but
not so bad. The daily toilet begins. Getting into the tub a
chore. Radio unheard while she blow-dries her hair. Make-up
and then dress. Help may be needed with shoes and
stockings. A politician in the news roundly cursed. Treats for
the cats before leaving for work.

> second hip replaced
> she spreads her legs
> with joy

Holidays

My wife is convalescing from surgery. Two daughters visit in shifts. One the week before Christmas. One the week after. In addition to everything else, they make these days festive, cheery. This despite the relentless rain. A third daughter not present makes herself felt.

> scattered body parts
> of gingerbread men
> the box marked fragile

Come the Revolution

Friday night. My wife and I are having drinks. We talk about our younger days. Before we knew each other. She takes me back . . .

Detroit. Mid-sixties. LaSalle and Lafayette, two fine-looking young men. Twins. Black Panthers. A young woman. Radical, white. They share a pitcher of beer.

"Come the revolution, we have to kill you."

Nods all around.

> glass crunches
> under rioters' feet
> motown smokin'

Commute

I ride the train to work. My fellow passengers tend to be nondescript. People-watching affords little amusement. So, I read. Today I leave my seat early and stand by the door to await my stop.

> low-cut dress
> can't keep my eyes off
> her reflection

Double Jeopardy

My wife is going for tests prior to surgery. As she pulls off the highway, there's an obstacle in the exit lane. She stops short. Bam! Rear-ended.

She's had her surgery. The repair shop is accommodating. When it's fixed, they'll bring her car to our home. The phone. As the driver pulls out of the shop, bam! Rear-ended.

> knee-deep
> the weatherman predicts
> more snow

Beach House

Half Moon Bay. A foghorn in the distance. Earlier sky and sea were gray. Now some clouds are white with patches of blue. The water is still gray-green but with a band of blue on the horizon. Here where the bay is protected by jetties, the water ripples in the wind. On the other side of the jetty, the sea is livelier. Small waves froth.

Seagulls line the shore. Someone walks a pair of dogs along the beach. They tear after the gulls, chase them away. The gulls gather further down the shore. Indoors a log burns in the fireplace. I return to finish my morning coffee.

> crossword finished
> we put the newspaper
> in the trash unread

Lost and Found
for Glenn

In the city on business. Dinner at a posh restaurant with an associate. Four queens at the next table. Flirting outrageously. They leave, dropping something at my feet. I retrieve it and turn to find them gone. It's a small canister, the sort that holds film. There are a couple of joints inside. When we leave, I give it to the maitre d'. He opens it and says, "Nice tip."

> taking the stairway
> one step at a time
> AA meeting

A Private Affair

Her voice booms through our work area. Despite the closed door. An argument with her lover. On and on. We strain not to hear. Suddenly her voice softens. The reconciliation is a private affair.

daybreak
two contrails meet
in a cloud of pink

The Interview
for Meghan

Our middle daughter is bright, pretty, successful. Nowadays even first dates include what she calls "the interview." She's on such a date now.

He asks about her first marriage, "Whose fault was the divorce?" She's vague, thinking but not saying, *none of your business*. He asks about family. "Do they pressure you to remarry, to have children?" He has done his homework. "Tell me about your dog Patches." And, "Why are you taking Japanese classes?"

He's from Eastern Europe on a temporary work permit. "But I can stay if I get married." He punches her playfully on the arm.

> turkey dinner
> getting the short end
> of the wishbone

Needs

My two-year-old grandson Sparky holds out his arms. I pick him up and he reaches for a nearby shelf.

"Ah, the desire to be held was a subterfuge," I say.

"Remember Maslow's hierarchy of needs," my son says. "Maybe he really did want to be held. Once that desire was satisfied, other possibilities opened up to him."

> earthworm
> she drops the twig
> for nesting

Winter's Approach

A carpet of browns and yellows. Birch leaves. Some dark around the edges. Like ancient parchment. The rain has stopped. But not the fall of leaves.

> indian summer
> the smoke I exhale
> is just that

Depth Perception

Mom is talking about being a young girl in North Miami.
Swimming in the canals. There were reports of alligators.
When she says, "The canals were bottomless," we demur.
Her face reddens. She moves on to talk of staying away from
the rock quarries. "They really were bottomless." Gales of
laughter. Hands over her face can't hide the redness.

> starry night
> my reach only
> arm's length

Keys

Family is gathered in Florida for spring break. My wife Bridget and granddaughter Alex go for a walk. It's Sunday and shops are closed. Alex sees one she wants to go into. She's two and a half and not easily deterred.

"Open it," she says.

"It's locked, honey," Bridget replies.

"You have keys." And nothing will do but to try them all.

"Mommy has keys," Alex says as they walk away.

> ice cream truck
> we all reach for
> our cell phones

Anniversary Getaway

Half Moon Bay. Morning coffee savored on the patio off our room. Squawk and yip of gull and tern. Foghorn in the distance. Diminishing drone of a pair of motorboats as they slip through a gap in the jetty. Waves gently lap the shore.

      to-do list
      she puts make love
      before lunch

Seasons

Their mother lives with one of my wife's sisters. A wedding invitation arrives in the mail.

"I don't have to go. I don't know them."

The sister patiently explains, "It's your granddaughter who's getting married."

"I don't have to go. They didn't go to my wedding."

> dry creek bed
> the weeping willow
> bowed down

Submission

As soon as I hit **Send**, I start imagining the rejection letter.

Dear Sir or Madam, With regard to the, ahem, poems you sent, we won't be using any of them, but rest assured that if we ever do develop a taste for crap, you will be at the top of our list. Sincerely yours, etc.

    tearing a leaf
    from my notebook
    a blaze in the fireplace

A Friend in Need

I had no idea. I knew of the difficult divorce, the separation from his children. Yet I had no idea. We talked from time to time of things large and small. But I had no idea. More than once, he tried to lift me out of my own doldrums. And I had no idea.

> a gentle breeze
> gathers itself and
> snuffs the candle out

Mother

"You don't know our ways," she says. And after seventy-two years of marriage, who would? She won't hear our advice. She won't know Dad's decline, though she does know it. She saw his mother's backward journey, her death in diapers.

> *I don't want to play in your yard,*
> *I don't like you anymore.*

And now they both go to a place, a home, not a home. And Mother chooses death. She will not abide homelessness, helplessness.

> unhinged
> the one-way sign
> points down